FIESTA!

D0120908

ISRAEL

W
FRANKLIN WATTS
NEW YORK • LONDON • SYDNEY

First published 1998
This edition first published 2001

Franklin Watts
96 Leonard Street
London EC2A 4XD

0 7496 4031 6

Dewey Decimal Classification Number: 394.2

A CIP catalogue record for this book is available from the British Library

Copyright © 1997 Times Media Pte Ltd, Singapore

Originated by Marshall Cavendish Books
an imprint of Times Media Pte Ltd
Times Centre, 1 New Industrial Road, Singapore 536196

Second Printing 2001

Marshall Cavendish Limited
Editorial Staff
Editorial Director: Ellen Dupont
Art Director: Joyce Mason
Designer: Melissa Stokes
Sub-Editors: Susan Janes, Judy Fovargue
Production: Craig Chubb
Editorial Assistant: Bindu Mathur

Crafts devised and created by Susan Moxley
Music arrangements by Harry Boteler
Photographs by Bruce Mackie

Printed in Italy

Adult supervision advised for all crafts and recipes
particularly those involving sharp instruments and heat.

CONTENTS

ISRAEL

To the east of the Mediterranean Sea, Israel is the land where the events in the Holy Bible of the Jews and Christians took place.

▶ **Jerusalem**, the capital, is a holy city for Christians, Jews and Muslims. The Dome of the Rock is a Muslim shrine.

◀ **The Wailing Wall** in Jerusalem is the most holy shrine of Judaism, the Jewish religion. Solomon, the third king of Israel, built a temple there 3,000 years ago. Part of the temple lay where the wall now stands. It became the custom for Jews to pray at the wall. They weep and wail while they ask God to be good to them.

Syria

Hefa (Haifa)

Teverya (Tiberias)

Sea of Galilee

Nazareth

Mediterranean Sea

WEST BANK

Tel Aviv Yafo (Jaffa)

Jordan

JERUSALEM

Bethlehem

Qiryat Gat

Gaza

GAZA STRIP

Hebron

Dead Sea

Be'er Sheva' (Beersheba)

ISRAEL

Jordan

Egypt

Elat

▲ **Avocados** grow in Israeli orchards. Israel exports fruit to countries all over the world.

▼ **This menorah** has seven branches. Menorahs like this one were used in synagogues thousands of years ago.

RELIGIONS

The main religion of Israel is the faith of Judaism. Israel is the only Jewish country in the world.

JUDAISM is thousands of years old. Its followers are called Jews and can be found all over the world.

Jewish people believe that they have been given the special task of spreading God's message throughout the world.

The holy book of Judaism is called the *Torah*. It is known as the Jewish bible and contains many of the religious laws and rules that Jews follow.

Jewish places of worship are called *synagogues*. Jews go there to meet and to pray at services led by a *rabbi*, or Jewish priest. Rabbis spend their lives studying Jewish scriptures and working with their congregations.

The holy day of the week in Judaism is Saturday and is called the

This is the Star of David, an important Jewish symbol. The Star of David appears on the national flag of Israel.

Sabbath. However, it begins when the sun goes down on Friday and ends when the sun sets the next day. Festival days also start and finish at sunset.

Some Jews eat according to strict rules. Food should be prepared in a special way, and some foods cannot be eaten at all. Food that follows these rules is called *kosher*.

Some Jewish people follow all their religious laws very closely. They are known as Orthodox Jews. Others have decided some laws are more important to modern life than others. They are Conservative or Reform Jews.

Throughout history Jewish people have suffered much hardship. For most of the last 2,000 years they have not had a country but lived all over the world among other religions. In some of these places the Jewish religion was not tolerated. In this century millions of European Jews were killed by the Nazis in Germany. This dreadful tragedy is known as the Holocaust.

After the Holocaust Jewish people finally got a country of their own. The nation of Israel was established in 1948. Many Jews have gone to live there, but many others remain in other countries around the world.

GREETINGS FROM **ISRAEL!**

Israel has a population of just over five million. Most are Jewish, but there are also some Christians and Muslims living there. One official language in Israel is Hebrew, an ancient Jewish language. Hebrew is read from right to left. Most Jewish religious writings are in Hebrew. The other official languages are English and Arabic. This last language is spoken by most of the countries that border Israel. Some Jewish people in Israel also speak Yiddish. It is a mixture of Hebrew, Polish and German. It developed among Jews who lived in Europe.

How do you say...

Hello

Shalom

Goodbye

L'hit ra'ot

Thank you

Todah

Peace

Shalom

ROSH HASHANAH

This holiday falls in September or October. It is a celebration of the Jewish New Year. It is also a time to remember the creation of the world and the story of Abraham.

Rosh Hashanah celebrates the beginning of the Jewish New Year. It is the first of the Ten Days of Repentance. It is a time when all Jews think about their behaviour and actions of

The shofar, or ram's horn, is blown at Rosh Hashanah. It has a long wailing sound. It is a reminder of the story in the Torah of Abraham. He sacrificed a ram and saved the life of his son Isaac.

the past year. They pray to God and ask for forgiveness for anything bad they have done. They think about how they can improve themselves in the year to come.

Rosh Hashanah is also a time when all Jews remember the creation of the world. They believe that God made the world during Rosh Hashanah.

On the evening when Rosh Hashanah starts, Jews eat sweet foods such as sliced apples and *hallah* bread – shaped as a plait and dipped in honey. Everyone enjoys honey biscuits and sweet potato pudding. They eat these sweet foods in the hope that the New Year will be sweet and very happy. People

*Apples and sweet honey are eaten
for Rosh Hashanah.
This shawl on the right is worn
by men when prayers are said.*

wish their friends and their family *Shanah Tovah*, or Happy New Year.

Most Jews go to the synagogue and pray.

Inside the tefillin *below is a tiny scroll with a prayer written on it. It is worn on the arm by some when praying at morning services.*

The rabbi, or minister, wears white as a sign of purity to symbolize a clean beginning to the New Year. The wailing sound of the shofar, or ram's horn, fills the building. It is blown to honour a story in the Torah about Abraham, who was so obedient to God he nearly gave his son as a sacrifice to God. The sound of the shofar is a reminder to all Jews that they must try to follow God's laws and regret their own bad deeds.

YOM KIPPUR

Yom Kippur is the name given to the last day of the Ten Days of Repentance. It is also known as the Day of Atonement. Jews consider Yom Kippur to be the most important and holiest day of the year.

On Yom Kippur, as on Rosh Hashanah, adults do not go to work, and children have a holiday from school. People observe a fast for the whole day, which means they do not eat or drink anything from sunset to sunset. They spend the day at the synagogue praying and reading from the prayer book and the Torah. People believe that on Yom Kippur the gates of heaven are open, and all thoughts and prayers will be welcomed and heard by God.

In synagogues white curtains and covers are used to give a feeling of purity. The services finally come to an end at sunset with a lastl blast of the shofar.

SUKKOT

This is harvest time, and Jews think about the hungry days when their ancestors wandered in the wilderness.

People all over Israel celebrate this week-long holiday by building a hut with a leafy open roof. This is called a *sukkah*. The holiday is "Sukkot" – the plural of sukkah. In the yards of synagogues and of many homes a sukkah is built and then it is covered with leaves, branches and fresh fruit for the Sukkot holiday. Those people in apartment buildings in the city build a sukkah outside on their balconies.

For the seven days of Sukkot the family eats dinner and holds activities in the sukkah. Some people even sleep in them!

The sukkah recalls that long ago Jews lived in slavery in Egypt until God sent a man named Moses to lead them to freedom.

The Jewish people

Sukkot is a celebration of the harvest. The Zionists, pioneers who wanted to reclaim this part of the world for a new Jewish state, worked hard to farm this dry and arid land. Even now Israel depends on carefully planned water supplies to grow crops such as citrus fruit, avocados and pep-pers. Harvests are always a blessing.

followed Moses for forty years through the desert and they built sukkot for rest and shelter.

Sukkot also recall harvest time in ancient Israel, when farmers used to work all day in the fields. They would build a sukkah near their crops so they could watch over them. The sukkah is a sign of God's care and His love.

In the synagogue service are held for this festival. The interior is decorated with harvested fruits and plants. Branches of palm, willow and myrtle form a *lulav* when they are bound together. A fourth element is the *etrog*, a citrus fruit. The lulav is held in one hand, the etrog in the other while a blessing is recited. Fruit crops are vital to Israel so harvest is a very important time.

The lulav is made from plants mentioned in the Bible. Some believe that the branches and the etrog symbolize land and settlements, fruit and fertility. The sukkah is a symbol of wandering.

An etrog is a fruit similar to a lemon. It is often stored in a silver container that looks like a large egg cup. Jews try to find beautiful etrogs to use in the Sukkot service.

SIMKHAT TORAH

The Sukkot holiday ends with this festival. It is also known as Rejoicing of the Torah and is celebrated with lively festivities at synagogues throughout Israel.

All year long parts of the Torah have been read aloud at the synagogue. The Torah is the Jewish bible and contains stories and rules. It is a holy document for Jews.

On this day the last section of the Torah is read. Immediately the reading of the Torah starts again from the beginning to end again at the next Simkhat Torah..

The Rejoicing of the Torah is a noisy, colourful service. The scrolls of the Torah are carried around the synagogue seven times in a procession. There is singing and dancing. In Orthodox

The Torah is the Jewish holy book. It is written on a scroll and kept in a place called the Ark in the synagogue. Below, Orthodox men and boys rejoice at Simkhat Torah.

groups only the men and boys are allowed to dance with the scroll but everyone enjoys a *kiddush*, which is a light meal made up of cakes and drinks.

BUILD A SUKKAH

YOU WILL NEED
17 sticks or twigs
Florists' twine or pipe cleaners
Air-hardening clay
Water-based paints
Leaves or other greenery
Thin cotton string

Most families in Israel build a sukkah for the Sukkot holidays. You can make a model and decorate it with real leaves and fruit made from clay.

1 Cut 4 sticks into equal lengths for the 4 corner poles of the sukkah. Cut 5 sticks of equal length longer than this for the width of the roof and the base. And cut 8 sticks into the same length for the depth of the roof and sides of the sukkah. Make the frame of the sukkah by binding the 4 corner sticks to 4 sticks on the roof and 3 at the base. Finish the roof with the remaining sticks.

2 For the decorations take the clay and mould it into small shapes of fruit as seen here. You can use a pencil to

give the fruit some textured patterns. Be sure to thread through the string at the top of the fruit while it is still wet. Allow the fruit to dry, then paint with the water-based paints. Hang the fruit from the roof of the sukkah as shown on the left. Finish the sukkah by placing leaves or shrubbery on top of the roof.

CHANUKAH

This holiday is also known as the Festival of Lights. It falls in December. Candles are lit and people remember the story of Judah Maccabee who fought for the Jews in ancient times.

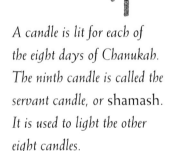

Chanukah lasts for eight days. Every Jewish home puts a *menorah*, or candlestick holder, in the window. One candle is lighted for each day of the festival until all are lit. People eat potato pancakes called *latkes*, and a doughnut called *sufganiyah*.

The origins of the celebration come from the acts of a brave man, Judah Maccabee, who fought against the Syrians over two thousand years ago. In Israel young people go to Modi'in, where Judah and his family lived. There they all light torches and have great bonfires in his honour.

A candle is lit for each of the eight days of Chanukah. The ninth candle is called the servant candle, or shamash. It is used to light the other eight candles.

Jews in different countries have developed their own particular cuisines. They mix local foods with traditional Jewish dishes. At the right is a doughnut called *koeksister* made by South African Jews for Chanukah. It is dripping with syrup and is extremely sweet and sticky.

DREIDEL

YOU WILL NEED
Coloured paper
4 pencils
Scissors
Black felt pen
Glue

1 Draw the shape below onto the coloured paper and cut out. On one side draw the black lines as pictured below. Poke a small hole at the centre of both the Xs on the square flaps on the left and right sides.

A *dreidel* is a spinning top used in a game for Chanukah. On each side of the top is a Hebrew letter which spells out "A great miracle happened there". This refers to the miracle of survival of the Jewish people and their temple all that time ago.

2 On the other side draw in the Hebrew characters on the four sides with a black felt pen. The characters are shown above on the right. Try to copy them as best as you can.

3 Fold the paper along the lines to make a box. Glue the flaps so the dreidel keeps its shape. Poke a pencil through the holes, and start play. Give everyone an equal number of tokens. Put one each into a pot. Spin the dreidel by turns. Look at the picture (left) to score. If the dreidel lands showing the letter drawn on the blue dreidel take half the tokens in the pot; if it shows the letter on the yellow dreidel, put in one token; if it shows the letter on the green one, no score; on the red, take the pot!

15

MIRACLE AT THE HOLY TEMPLE

Chanukah is a time when Jews remember the story of

Judah Maccabee. He won back the Holy Temple in Jerusalem

from the Syrian king over two thousand years ago. A legend has

grown round the battle for the Holy Temple.

A LONG TIME AGO the Israelites, which is what the early Jewish peoples were called, were involved in a terrible battle against the Syrian king, Antiochus. The king wanted all the Israelites in Israel to give up their religion. The king ordered his armies to conquer the great Holy Temple in Jerusalem. Hundreds of armed Syrian soldiers marched into the Temple and tore down all the objects, leaving the great temple in ruins.

The king was confident that he had beaten the Israelites. After all, he had thousands of strong men in his army. But a brave warrior named Judah Maccabee refused to give up the fight. He organized a small number of brave, strong men to fight fiercely against the Syrian king. With Judah Maccabee leading them, the small army of Israelites was able to beat the powerful king. They won and so could continue to keep the Jewish faith and people strong and alive.

The first thing the victorious Israelites did after their battle was to reclaim their Holy Temple. They repaired all the damage that the Syrian armies had done. At last, the work was done, and once again it was a Jewish temple. But when they hurried into the temple, they found that they only had enough oil to keep the lamps burning for just one day. The lamps were supported by a menorah, a special kind of holder. Next day when the Jews went to the temple, the lamps were still burning.

It happened again the next day and the day after that. Eight days passed and the lamps never lost their light or their oil. Somehow the lamps stayed burning for eight whole days. It was a miracle from God to bless the Israelites after their brave victory over the Syrians. The temple menorah held seven lamps, one for each day of the week. After this the design was changed to carry more.

Chanukah menorahs are candelabrum carrying nine symbolic candles. Eight of the candles are for each day that the lamps burned in the temple, and the ninth is the symbolic oil. It is used to light the other candles.

Tu Bishvat

This festival takes place in January or February. It is known as the New Year for trees. Jews throughout Israel plant trees and remember the importance of nature.

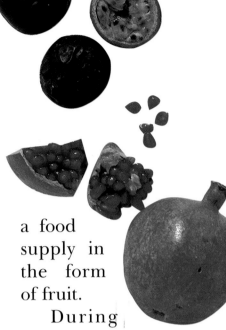

HUMMUS SANDWICHES

Flat pitta bread and creamy hummus, made from pounded chickpeas and sesame seed paste, are popular Israeli sandwich ingredients. You can buy hummus and pitta bread in supermarkets and delicatessens.

Cut a pitta bread in half across the middle, then open up each half to make pockets. Spoon in the hummus. Add other fillings to make delicious combinations. Try sliced tomatoes and onions, lettuce, olives and peppers. A perfect picnic dish!

a food supply in the form of fruit.

During the Tu Bishvat holiday schoolchildren from all over Israel travel into the countryside to plant trees. They recite a prayer or blessing as they are putting the tree into the ground. As they picnic the children always take time to

In the Jewish religion trees are an important symbol. Trees are thought of as representing life itself. In the Bible someone who does many good deeds is compared to a tree that bears a lot of fruit.

Trees are also very important in a hot, dry country like Israel. People need them for shade. The roots of trees prevent erosion of the land and they help the growth of other plants. And, of course, trees produce

HAVAH NAGILAH

Ha - vah — Na - gi - lah, Ha - vah — Na - gi - lah, Ha - vah — Na - gi - lah

ve - nis - me - chah! Ha - vah — Na - gi - lah, Ha - vah — Na - gi - lah,

Ha - vah - Na - gi - lah ve - nis - me - chah! Ha - vah ne - ran - ne - nah,

Ha - vah ne - ran - ne - nah, Ha - vah, ha - vah ne - ran - ne - nah!

Ha -vah ne-ran-ne-nah, Ha-vah ne-ran-ne-nah, Ha-vah, ha-vah ne - ran - ne nah!

HAVAH NAGILAH
Let's be happy. (twice)
Let's sing and be happy. (thrice)
Get up, get up brothers and sisters.
Get up brothers and sisters
with happy hearts. (four times)
Get up brothers and sisters
with happy hearts.

remember the great importance of nature.

Jewish people who live in other parts of the world donate money so that trees can be planted in Israel. There is a custom for parents to plant a tree for each new child that is born. Years later, branches from the tree may be used as wedding decorations when the child gets married.

On this holiday Spanish Jews have a special meal in which fruits are eaten in a particular order. First are those with a peel or shell: pistachio nuts or pomegranates. The second course has

fruits with a seed that cannot be eaten, such as grapes and dates, while the third course involves fruit that can be eaten whole like figs or seedless grapes.

PURIM

This lively festival takes place in February or March. It celebrates deliverance from a serious danger that threatened Jews long ago.

Purim recalls the story of Esther and how the Jewish people were saved from being killed by Haman. He was minister to the king of ancient Persia. The Jews' lives were spared thanks to the wife of the king,

This is a model of a rabbi. He is in the happy, joking mood of Purim. In the synagogues the rabbis read aloud the story of Purim from the Scroll of Esther, which is known as the Megillah.

Queen Esther, and her uncle Mordecai.

Purim is also a time to recall all the occasions when their enemies have tried to destroy the Jews.

But Purim is a happy celebration in Israel. People gather at the synagogue and listen to the story of Queen Esther. When evil Haman's name is

This very noisy rattle is called a greggor. People whistle, shout and shake the greggor to make a loud noise when Haman's name is heard during the story of Esther and Mordecai.

heard in the story, every listener shouts. Feet are stamped, and rattles are shaken to drown out the name. People cheer and clap when the heroic Esther and Mordecai are mentioned.

This is a time for charity, and the poor are given food and gifts. Friends give each other sweets and

20

sweet pastries called *hamentashen*, which are shaped to imitate Haman's hat.

Street parades are filled with children in fancy dress. The girls may dress as Esther, but others choose to go as clowns, gypsies or even spacemen. This street parade is known as *Ad-lo-yada*.

The Purim carnival is full of people wearing masks. There are also beauty contests, in which the contestants dress as Queen Esther in beautiful gowns.

CHICKPEAS WITH CARROTS

SERVES 4

1 large onion
2 small carrots
1 courgette
1 small potato
1 tbsp vegetable oil
1 tin (400g) chickpeas
2 tbsp sugar
½ tsp ground cinnamon
Flat-leaf parsley, to garnish

1 Preheat the oven to 200°C/400°F/Gas 6.
2 Peel and slice onion. Peel and grate carrots. Finely grate the courgette. Peel and grate potato.
3 Heat the oil in a large frying pan with an ovenproof handle and tight-fitting lid.
4 Add the onion and fry until golden brown, stirring often.
5 While onions are frying, open the chickpeas. Pour into a sieve

in the sink. Rinse and drain well.
6 Add chickpeas to pan. Stir in carrots, courgette and potato. Sprinkle with sugar and cinnamon and stir until blended.
7 Cover pan and place in the oven. Cook for 40 minutes until the potato is cooked through and all the vegetables are hot.
8 Wearing oven gloves, remove the pan. Cut into wedges and serve with sprig of parsley.

MORDECAI AND ESTHER

The festival of Purim celebrates the heroism of Queen Esther and her uncle Mordecai. The Jews have a long history of suffering because they will not give up their faith. This story helps strengthen this faith, and gives them the courage to stand together when faced with danger.

THOUSANDS OF YEARS AGO in the land of ancient Persia there lived a king named Ahasuerus. He lived quite happily in the palace with his wife, the beautiful Queen Esther.

The king had a prime minister who looked after the running of the land. The prime minister's name was Haman. Haman was very powerful, but he was also wicked and evil. Haman took any chance to force his power on people. For example Haman insisted that everyone should bow when he walked into the palace. But Mordecai, who was Queen Esther's uncle, refused to bow in front of the evil Haman. This made Haman angry.

Mordecai was Jewish and bowed only to God. Haman became so angry at Mordecai's refusal to bow that he decided to kill all the Persian Jews.

Haman set to work to carry out his evil plan. He needed the king to sign a royal order to have all the Jews in Persia executed.

So Haman was very sneaky. He persuaded the king to sign the royal order declaring the Jews were not loyal subjects. King Ahasuerus signed and sealed the document with his royal seal. He did not realize that in ordering the death of all Persian Jews his wife Esther would also be killed. Haman seemed to have succeeded in his plan to kill these people. Haman decided the date of the massacre by drawing lots, which is a kind of raffle or lottery. These lots are called *purim* in Hebrew.

Haman and his sons then built a gallows to hang Mordecai. Persian Jews were terrified as the date of doom grew near. But Mordecai and the king's wife, Queen Esther, were not going to let their fellow Jews die. They decided that they must find a way to stop the execution of the Jews.

In the days before the execution date Queen Esther hosted two grand banquets and invited her husband the king and the wicked Haman. Queen Esther knew of Haman's evil plot, but she didn't say anything to the king until the second banquet. Then she revealed to the king how Haman had tricked him into signing the royal order. The king was outraged to learn he had been fooled by his prime minister.

At once the king signed a new order saying Jews were allowed to defend themselves if they were attacked. Jews all over the land breathed a sigh of relief. Their lives had all been saved by the brave and beautiful Queen Esther.

Haman and his sons were hanged on the gallows they had built for Mordecai. The king then appointed Mordecai to be his prime minister in Haman's place and Esther ruled that these events be celebrated every year.

PESAKH

This spring festival is also called Passover. Jewish people remember and celebrate their freedom from slavery. It is a time when the family gathers to enjoy a special ceremonial meal together.

The Jews lived in ancient Egypt where they were slaves to the kings, or pharaohs. Jews were called the Children of Israel or Israelites. God promised to help the Israelite leader Moses and his people to escape from slavery.

After God's words Egypt suffered ten plagues. Finally the pharaoh begged the Israelites to leave and for their God to stop punishing the Egyptians. The festival of Pesakh celebrates this escape from slavery.

No crumbs must be in the house on this day, so homes are spring-cleaned. The family gathers at the table for a special meal called a *seder* and tells the story of Passover. The seder begins with the child who is youngest in the

The table is set for the seder with special dishes, glasses and cutlery. Some Jews keep these dishes separate from the rest, and bring them out once a year, for the Passover meal.

This special dish is placed in the middle of the table for the seder. It has individual compartments for all of the symbolic foods of the Passover holiday.

family asking why this night differs from others. The answers are read from the *Haggadah*, a book that tells the Passover story.

The foods served at the seder meal are thin, flat bread called *matzah* is eaten. The Israelites did not have time to let their bread rise when they fled from Egypt. A roasted egg and a bone

of lamb recall the beasts given to God as sacrifice. A dish of salt water is for the tears of the Israelite slaves in Egypt. *Charoset,* or *haroseth* made of nuts, apples and wine is for the cement used to build cities for the Egyptians. Everybody has glasses of wine to celebrate this event in Jewish history.

important and bitter herbs such as horse radish symbolize slavery. Parsley marks the coming of spring. A

THE PARTING OF THE WAVES

Every Passover Jews remember the story of the Israelites' flight from slavery in Egypt thousands of years ago. God chose a wise man named Moses to lead their escape. This is a story describing how God performed a miracle to help the Israelites reach the Promised Land.

MORE THAN THREE THOUSANDS YEARS ago Jewish people were called Israelites and lived as slaves of the pharaoh in Egypt. They were led by a man named Moses who tried often to get the pharaoh to grant his people freedom. Finally the pharaoh agreed to release the slaves. He told Moses to take all the Israelites out of Egypt.

The Israelites were overjoyed. They were finally free! And they had a wise leader like Moses who was going to take them to a new country where they could live in peace and worship their God – the Promised Land.

The Israelites started their long journey to the Promised Land. But then the pharaoh changed his mind and decided that he wanted the Israelites to return to be his slaves again. He sent an army to bring them back to Egypt.

Moses and the Israelites could hear the sound of the army's chariots getting closer and closer. They grew very scared. Moses told them to have faith that God would see them safely to the Promised Land.

The Israelites were running to try to escape the pharaoh's rapidly approaching army. They finally came to the banks of the mighty Red Sea. The Israelites were desperate. They had no boats to cross the sea. The waves were far too strong for them to try to swim across. They were trapped and feared they would be captured by the Egyptian army.

But Moses reminded them to have faith in God. He then raised his walking stick and pointed it into the Red Sea. There was a huge roaring wind. The waves frothed and thundered.

The Israelites were amazed to see the sea split in two, with a broad path running in between. The waves stayed high and still. It was a miracle!

They followed Moses across the path, with its huge walls of waves rising on either side. They all rushed along the dry path to the other side of the Red Sea. The last Israelite had scarcely crossed when the Egyptian army arrived at the banks of the Red Sea. The soldiers ran into the path. The waves came crashing down, and the Egyptian soldiers were drowned. The Israelites were safe, thanks to God, and they had learnt to trust God to lead them to the Promised Land.

YOM HA'ATZMA'UT

This holiday is also known as Independence Day. On this day Israelis celebrate the anniversary of the founding of the state of Israel in 1948.

Israel became a country on May 14, 1948. The Jewish people had not had their own country in almost 2,000 years.

Before the new nation of Israel was founded, Jews all over the world hoped that one day they could have their own country again.

About a hundred years ago, some

This is the word shalom written in Hebrew. It means peace. One of the state of Israel's official symbols is the olive branch of peace.

Jews from Europe moved to what is now Israel. They lived in farming communities called *kibbutzim*. These Jews belonged to a group called Zionists. The goal of Zionists was to form a country for Jewish people. They worked hard for

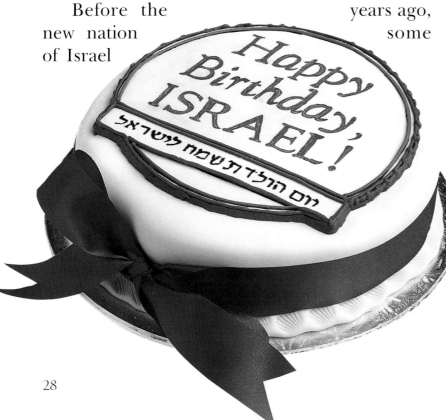

Jews all over the world make a "birthday" cake on each anniversary of the founding of the state of Israel.

years to convince the world they should have their own country. When millions of Jews were killed in the Holocaust, European and American governments decided Jews should have a land they could call their own. That is how the state of Israel was born.

When Israel was founded in 1948, neighbouring Arab countries were not happy. They declared war on Israel. So now on the day before Independence Day, Israelis hold a Remembrance Day holiday to honour those who have lost their lives fighting for Israel.

A loud siren is heard to mark the start of celebrations on Independence Day. There are fireworks, parades and singing and dancing in the streets. People sing the national anthem called *Ha-Tikvah*, meaning "hope" in Hebrew. They pray to thank God for giving the Jewish people their own land.

HA–TIKVAH

Kol — od ba-lei-vav pe-ni-mah
ne-fesh ye-hu-di ho-mi-yah ule-
fa-a-tei — miz-rah ka-di-mah
a-yin le Tzi-yon tzo-fi-yah.

As long as in our hearts,
there is a Jewish spirit,
And towards the east,
our eyes turn to Zion –
Our hope is not lost.
The hope of 2,000 years.
To be a free nation,
in our own land.
In the land of Zion,
in Jerusalem.

OTHER FESTIVALS

Before 1948 Israel was called Palestine. It is also known as the "Holy Land" because this is where Judaism, Islam and Christianity have their roots.

THE NIGHT OF THE ASCENSION is celebrated by Muslims on the fifth day of the seventh month. This is according to the Islamic calendar, which follows the cycles of the moon. Mohammed ascended into heaven on this date. He was standing on a great rock in Jerusalem when this happened. A mosque was built to protect the rock, which can still be seen. The mosque (see model on right) is called the Dome of the Rock. Pilgrims come to worship here. On the Night of the Ascension they crowd into this sacred site.

EASTER in Israel brings Christian pilgrims from all over the world. This is the most solemn date in the Christian calendar. It marks the Crucifixion and the Resurrection of Jesus Christ. Jesus was forced to carry His cross through the streets of Jerusalem to the Hill of Calvary. Christians re-enact his journey with people playing the parts of Jesus, the Disciples and others who were involved. The events on the journey are known as the Stations of the Cross, and images showing these events (left) are found in many churches. Everything that happened on the journey is acted out each year. The players are followed by thousands of Christians who have come to Jerusalem to remember Jesus' suffering.

There are a number of Christian communities in Israel. They represent the various sections of Christianity: Roman Catholic, Orthodox and Protestant.

WORDS TO KNOW

Ark: The special cabinet in a synagogue that contains the five sacred scrolls of the Torah.

Atonement: The act of making up for one's wrong-doing.

Deliverance: Being rescued from danger.

Erosion: Loss of soil caused by the action of wind and water.

Fast: To go without food deliberately.

Fertility: The ability to produce plentiful crops.

Holocaust: The murder of millions of European Jews and other minority groups by the Nazis during World War II.

Kibbutz: An Israeli farming community that is owned and run by its members.

Kosher: Having to do with food that meets the strict rules and regulations of Jewish law.

Miracle: A remarkable event thought to be caused by a super-human power.

Palestine: The name given to the land of Israel before it became a Jewish state in 1948.

Plague: An unusual attack of disease, insects or pests thought to be sent by God as a punishment.

Rabbi: A Jewish religious leader and teacher.

Repentance: The act of feeling sorry for one's wrongful behaviour.

Ritual: A religious ceremony that must be performed in a certain way or order.

Scriptures: Holy writings.

Synagogue: A Jewish place of worship.

Torah: The Jewish bible, the Five Books of Moses, which contain many of the religious laws and rules that Jews follow. The Torah is handwritten on scrolls.

ACKNOWLEDGMENTS

WITH THANKS TO:

Nilgün Atalay, dress p21, Rabbi J.Black, Manor House Media, London shofar, tefill-in, shawl p8-9, etrog container, lulav p10-11, Torah p12, candelabra p14-15, gregor p20, chalice, candlesticks p24-25. Vale Antiques, London cartoon p12-13, rabbi model p20, peace medallion p29, Catholic Truth Society, London icon p30.

PHOTOGRAPHS BY:

All photographs by Bruce Mackie except: John Elliott p21(bottom). Cover photograph by Pictor International.

ILLUSTRATIONS BY:

Alison Fleming title page, p4-5, Mountain High Maps ® Copyright © 1993 Digital Wisdom, Inc. p4-5. Alison Fleming p6. Tracy Rich p7. Robert Shadbolt p17. Philip Bannister p23. Adam Hook p27.

INDEX